HAL LEONARD *MORE* EASY BANJO SOLOS

BY MAC ROBERTSON

T0088366

Welcome to *More Easy Banjo Solos*, a collection of 16 timeless songs arranged for 5-string banjo. This beginner's songbook can be used on its own or as a supplement to the *Hal Leonard Banjo Method*, or any other beginning banjo method. The songs are arranged in order of difficulty and presented in an easy-to-follow format.

Every song in the book includes a full audio demo track of the banjo arrangement along with guitar or banjo accompaniment. Use the access code below to unlock the audio demo tracks online, for download or streaming!

To access audio visit:
www.halleonard.com/mylibrary

Enter Code
3161-8494-3708-4026

The author gratefully acknowledges Jon Peik's assistance with arrangements and accompaniment.
Recording credits: Mac Robertson – banjo, bass, and guitar; Jon Peik – guitar and banjo

ISBN 978-1-4803-0923-4

HAL•LEONARD®
CORPORATION
7777 W. BLUEMOUND RD. P.O. BOX 13819 MILWAUKEE, WI 53213

Visit Hal Leonard Online at
www.halleonard.com

JAMBALAYA
(On the Bayou)

Words and Music by
Hank Williams

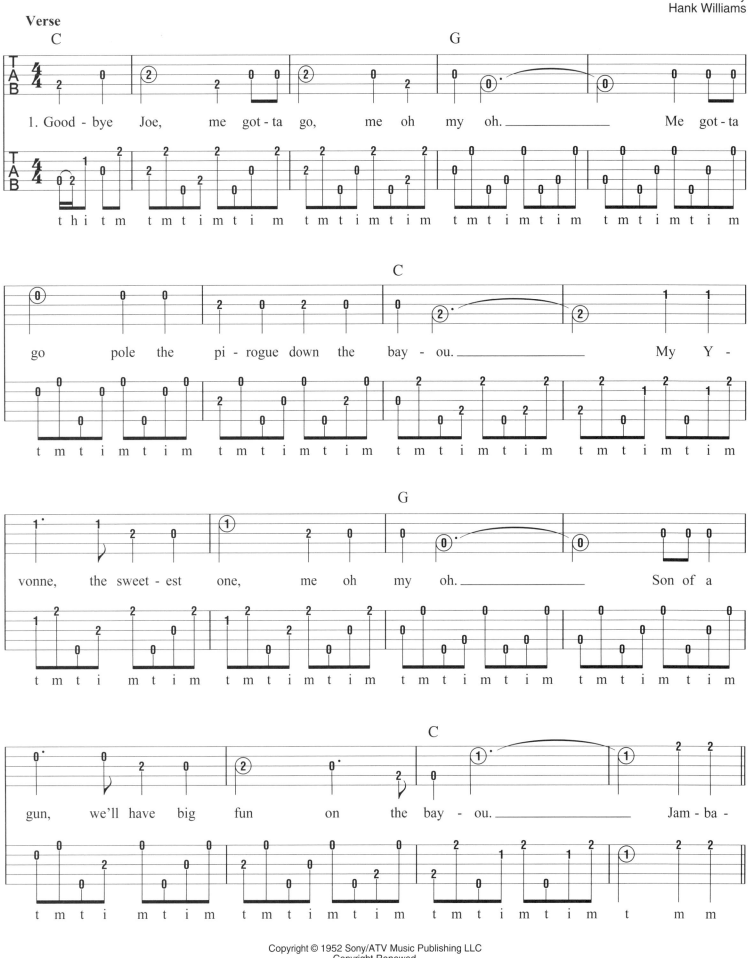

Chorus

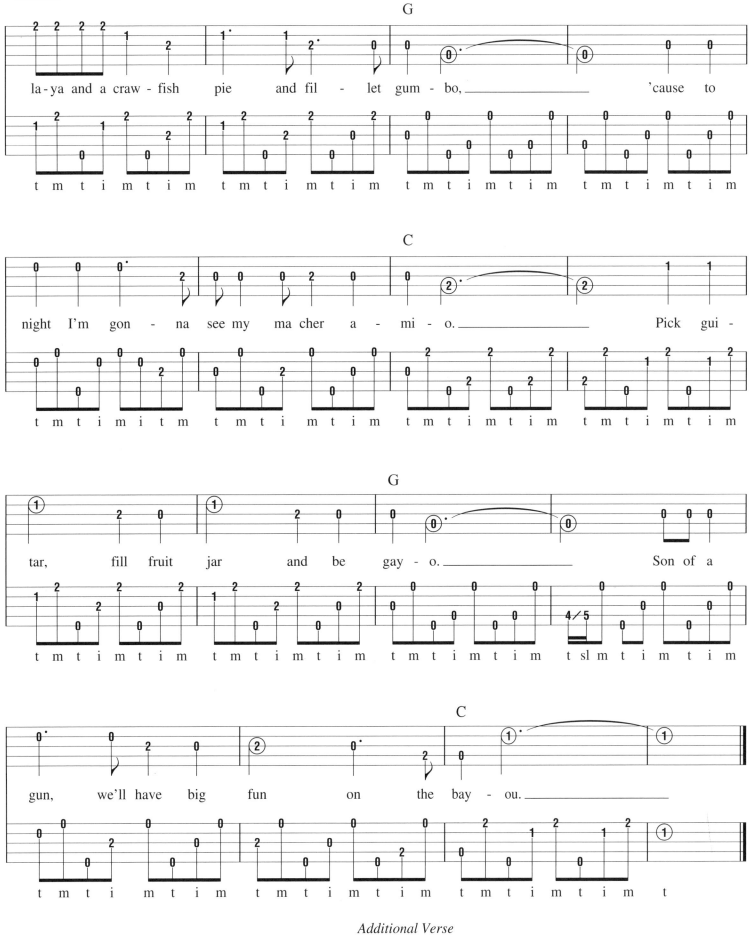

Additional Verse

2. Thibodaux, Fontaineaux the place is buzzin',
   Kinfolk come to see Yvonne by the dozen.
   Dress in style and go hog wild, me oh my oh.
   Son of a gun we'll have big fun on the bayou. *CHORUS*

3

CORNBREAD AND BUTTER BEANS

Words and Music by Dominique Flemons,
Rhiannon Giddens Laffan and Thomas Justin Robinson

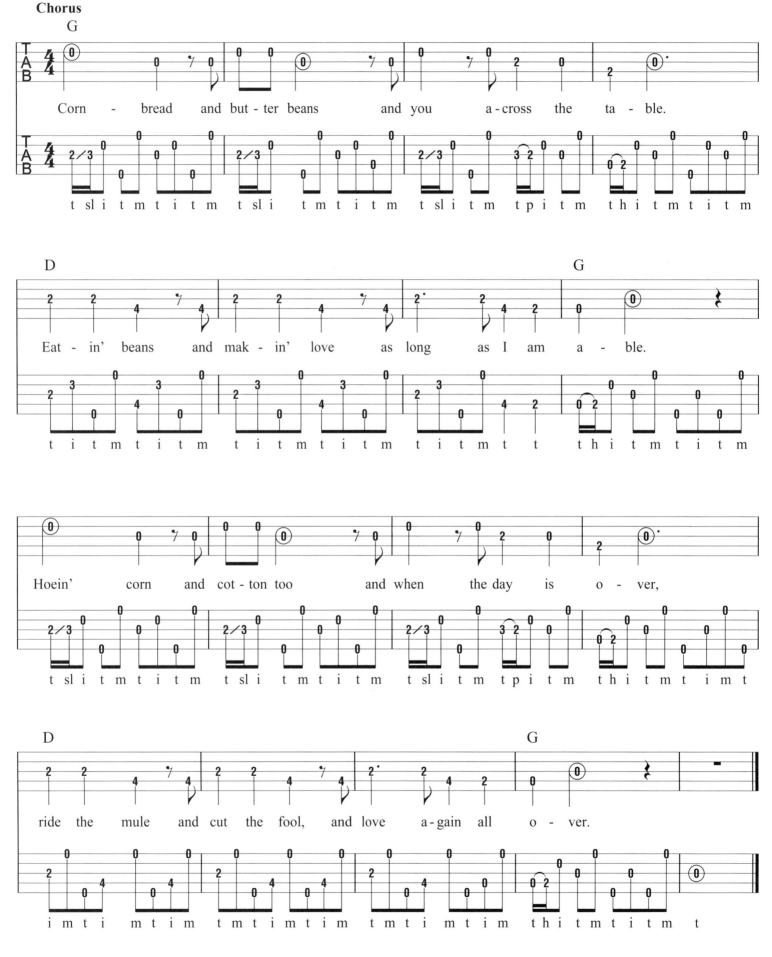

YOUR LOVE IS LIKE A FLOWER

By E. Lilly, Lester Flatt and Earl Scruggs

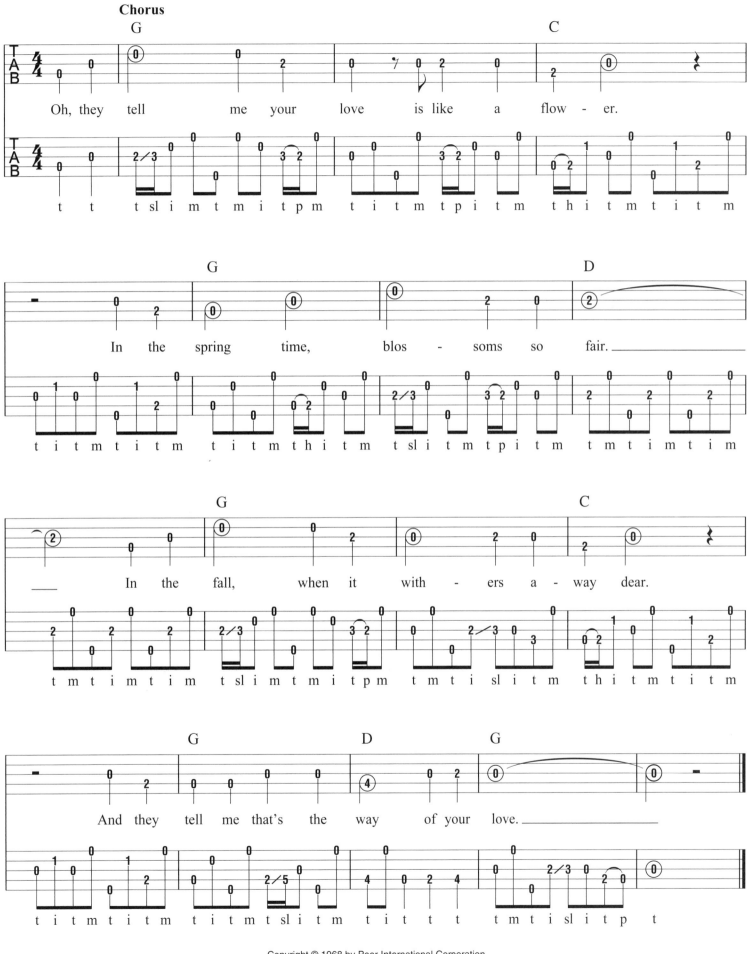

BIG SANDY RIVER

By Bill Monroe and Kenny Baker

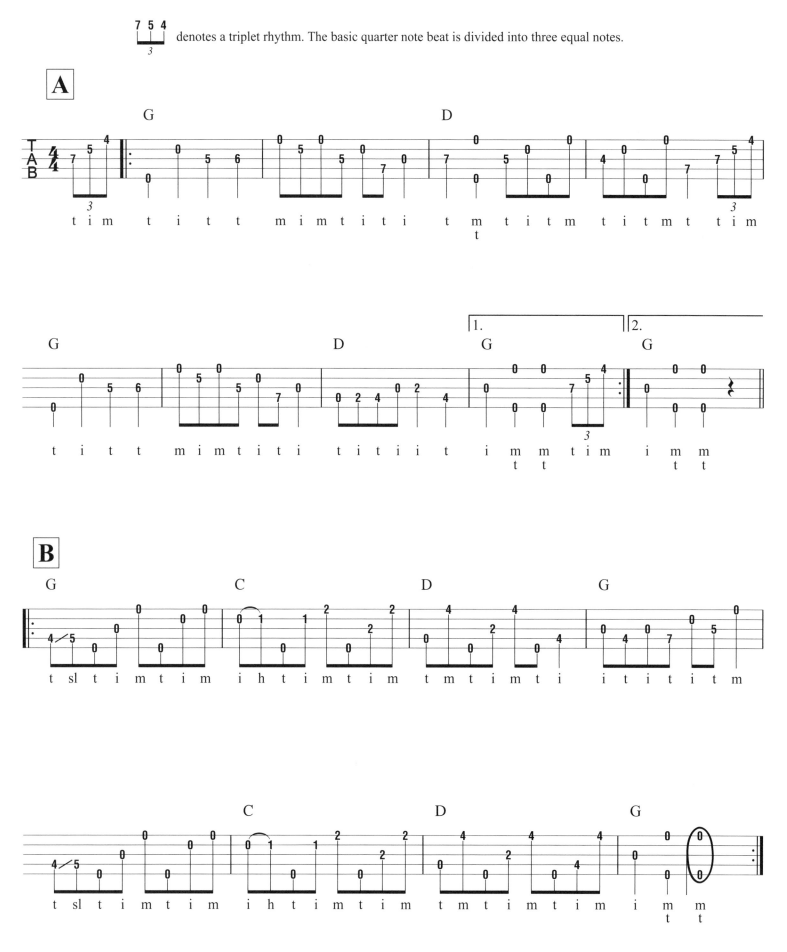

I'M SO LONESOME I COULD CRY

Words and Music
by Hank Williams

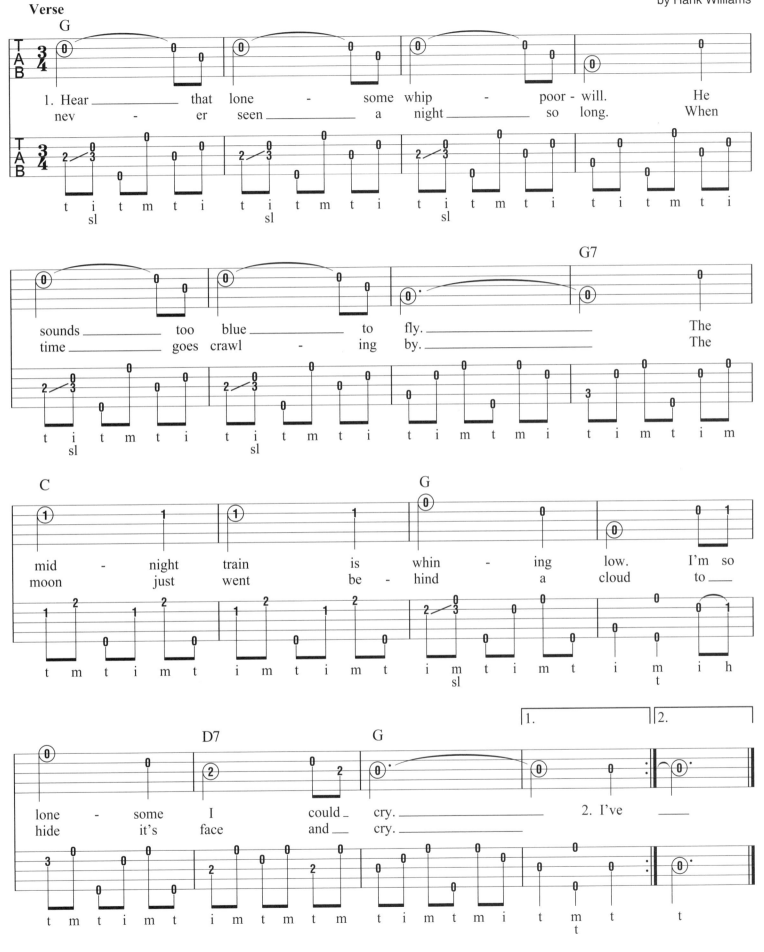

I AM A MAN OF CONSTANT SORROW

Words and Music by
Carter Stanley

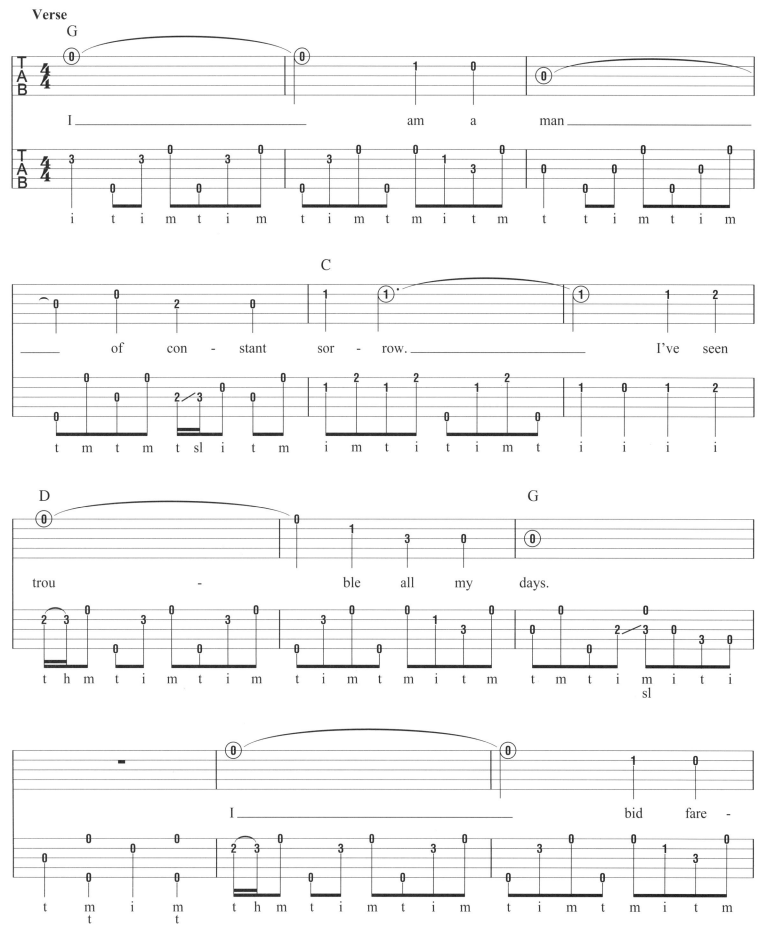

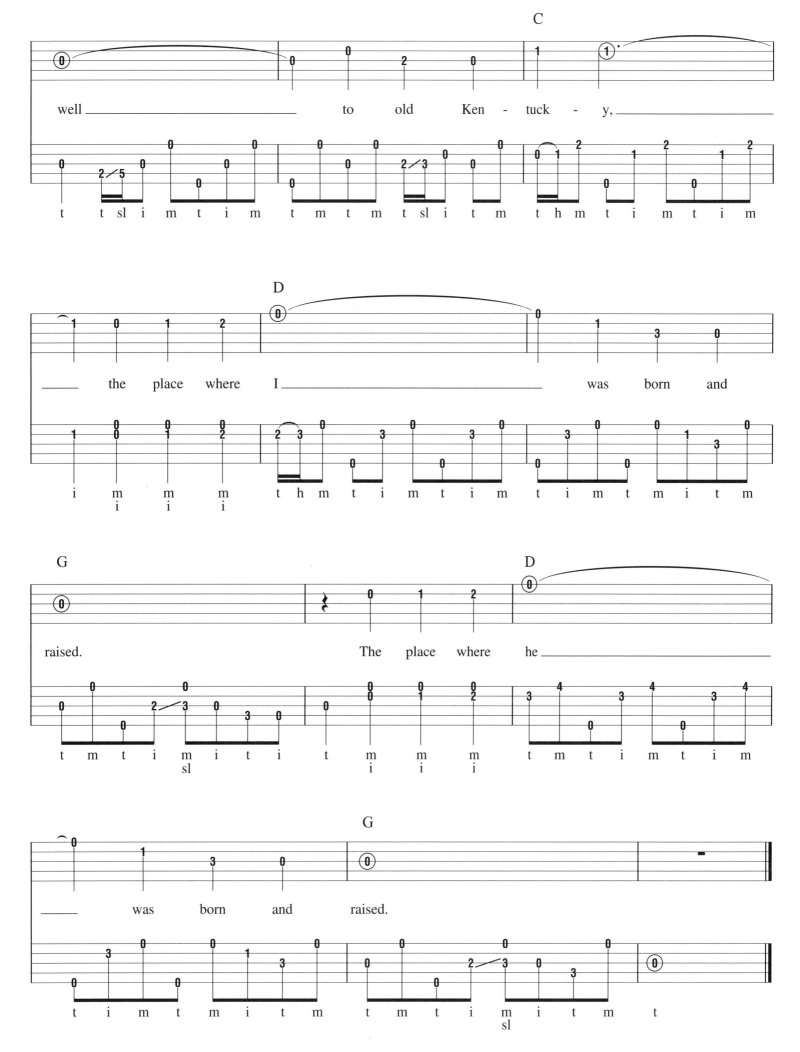

ABILENE

Words and Music by Lester Brown,
John D. Loudermilk and Bob Gibson

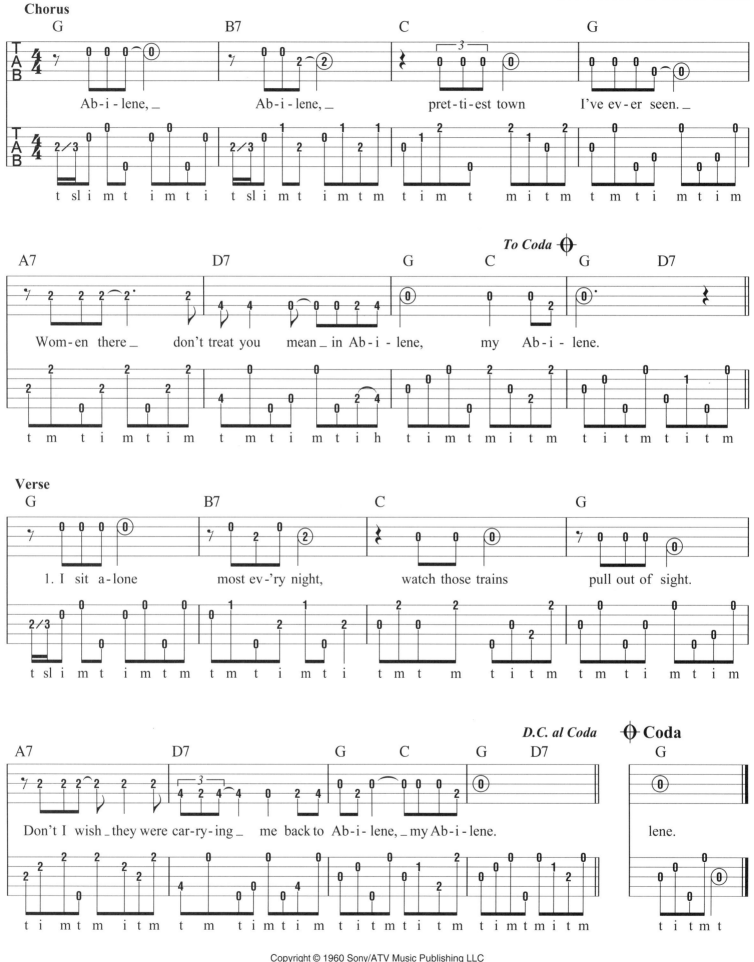

FREIGHT TRAIN

Words and Music by
Elizabeth Cotten

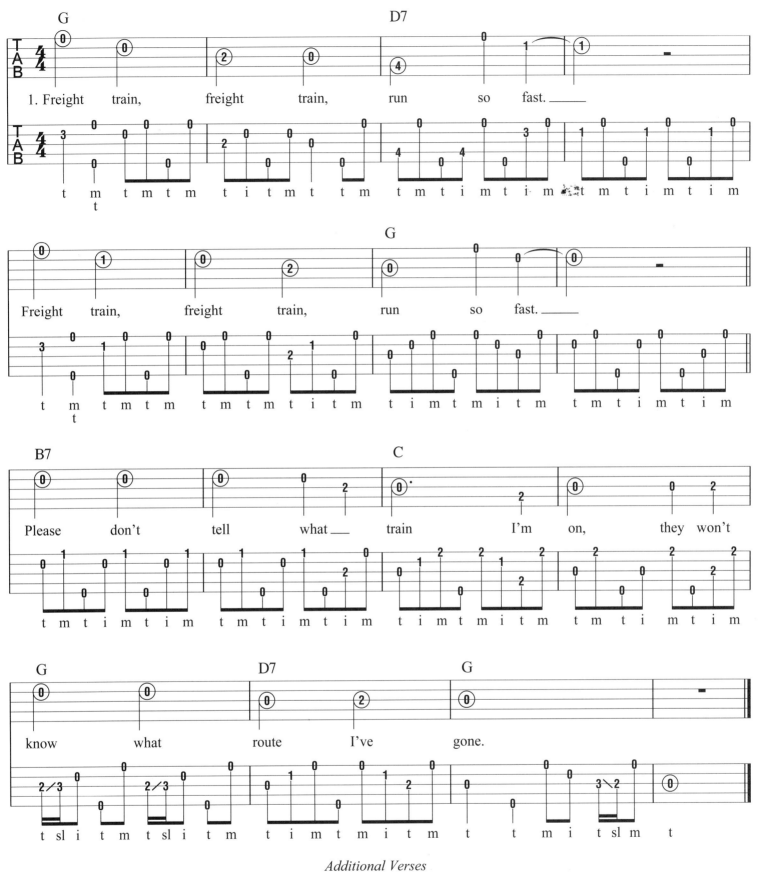

Additional Verses

2. When I'm dead and in my grave,
No more good times here I'll crave.
Place the stones at my head and feet
And tell them I've gone to sleep.

3. When I die, Lord, bury me deep,
Way down on old Chestnut Street,
So I can hear old Number Nine
As she comes rolling by.

WORDS UNSPOKEN

Words and Music by Steve Martin
and Peter Wernick

Open D Tuning:
*(5th-1st) A-D-F#-A-D

A

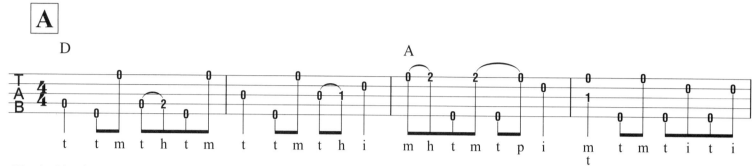

*For the 5th string, use a 5th-string capo or tune it up one whole step.

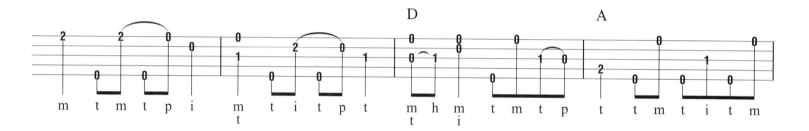

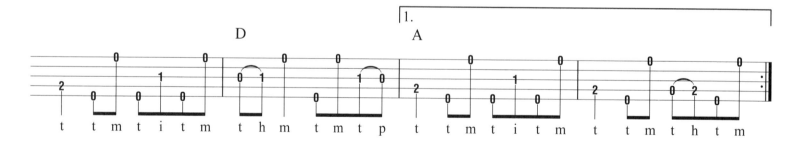

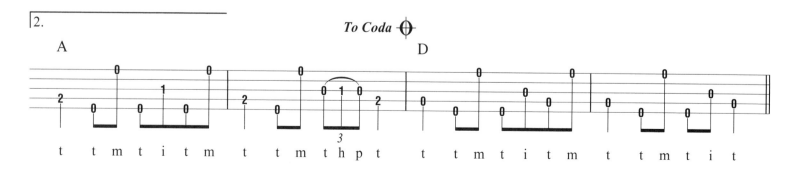

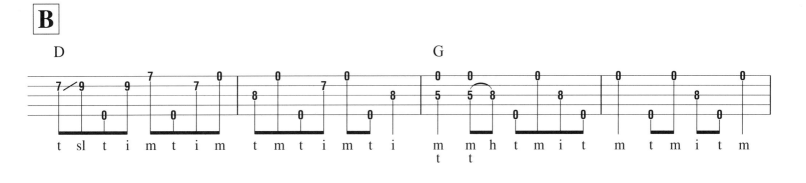

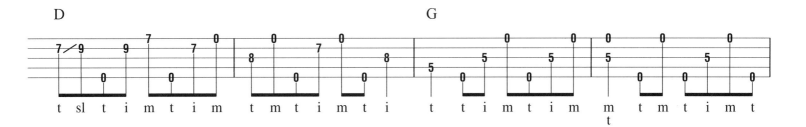

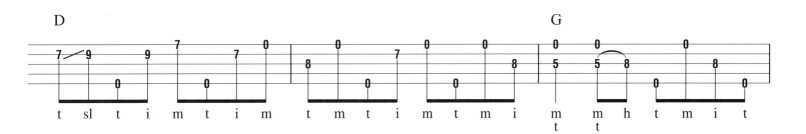

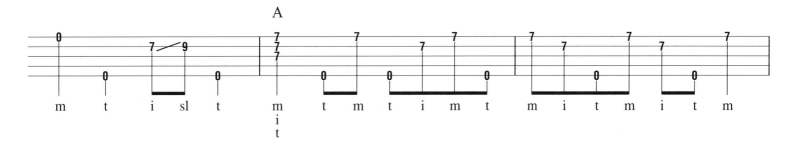

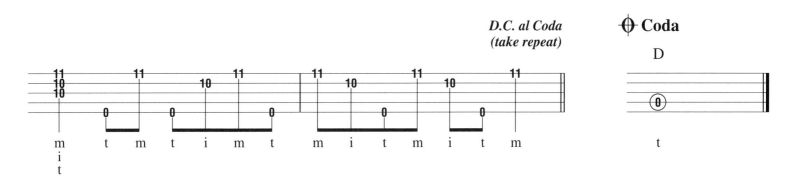

DOUG'S TUNE
(My Grass Is Blue)

Words and Music by
Douglas Dillard

Place the left hand fingers in this pattern to begin the song:

At measure three use this fingering:

Reminder: indicates a fret hand pull-off.

indicates that the notes are tied together.

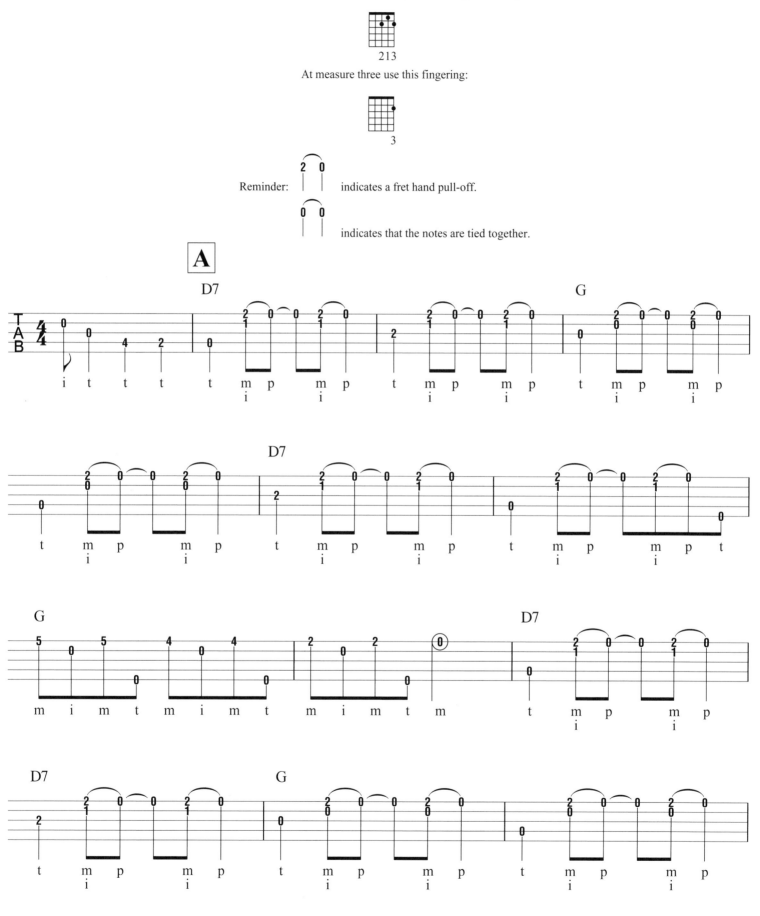

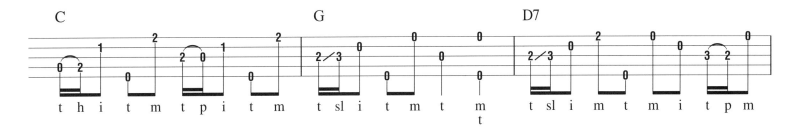

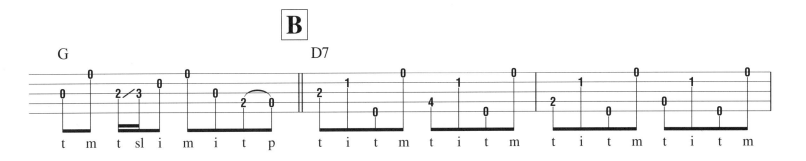

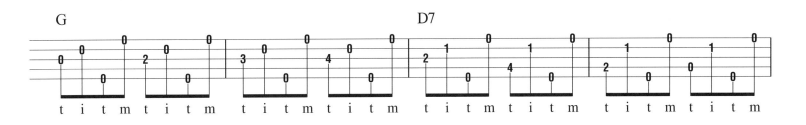

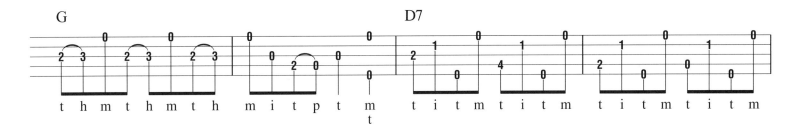

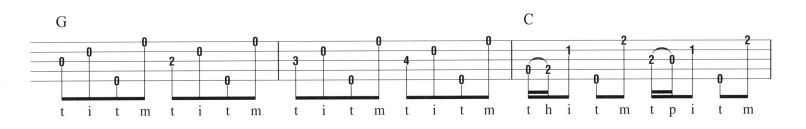

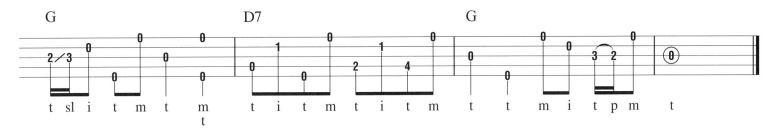

RED WING

Words by Thurland Chattaway
Music by Kerry Mills

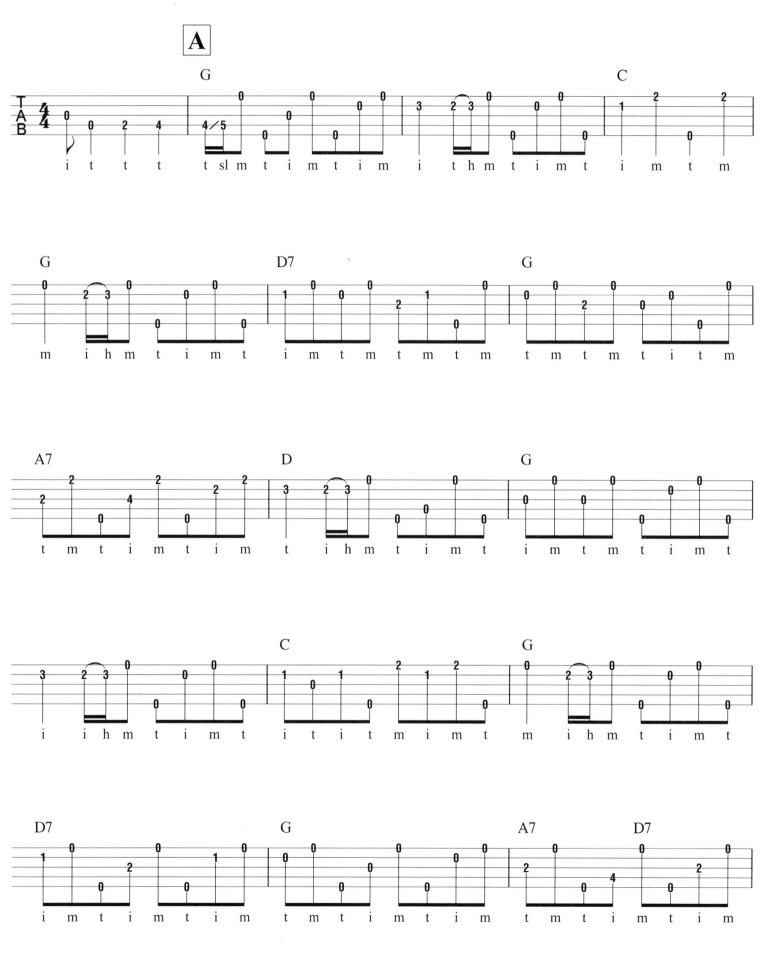

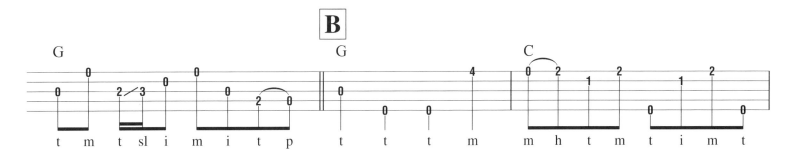

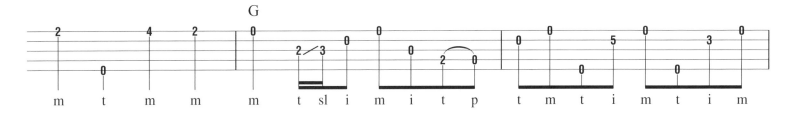

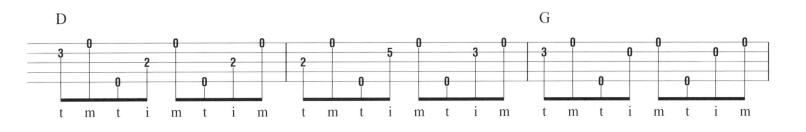

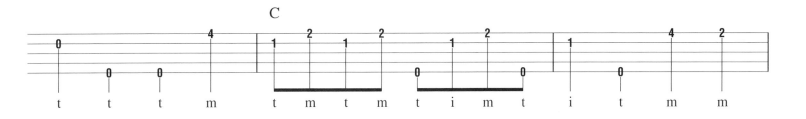

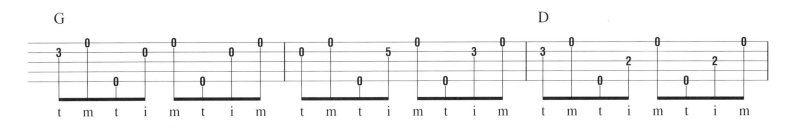

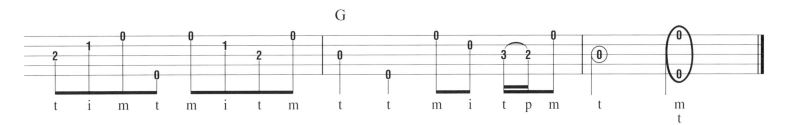

BLACKBERRY BLOSSOM

Traditional

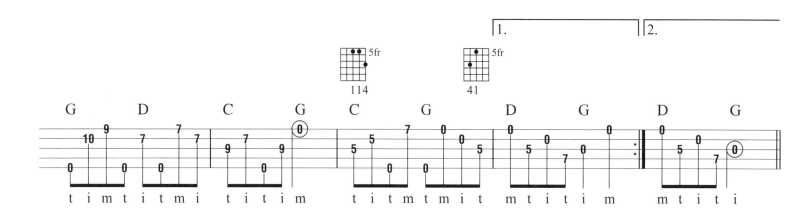

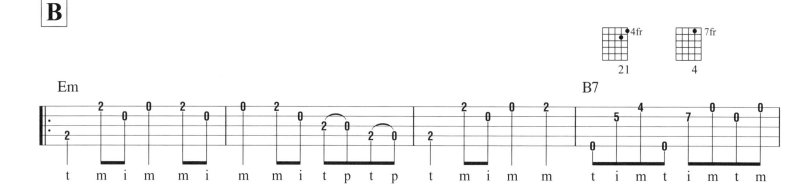

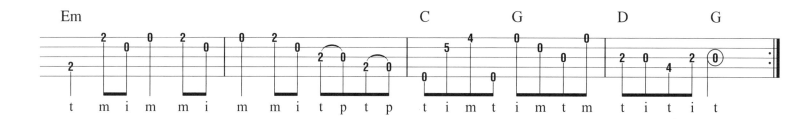

BLUE MOON OF KENTUCKY

Words and Music by
Bill Monroe

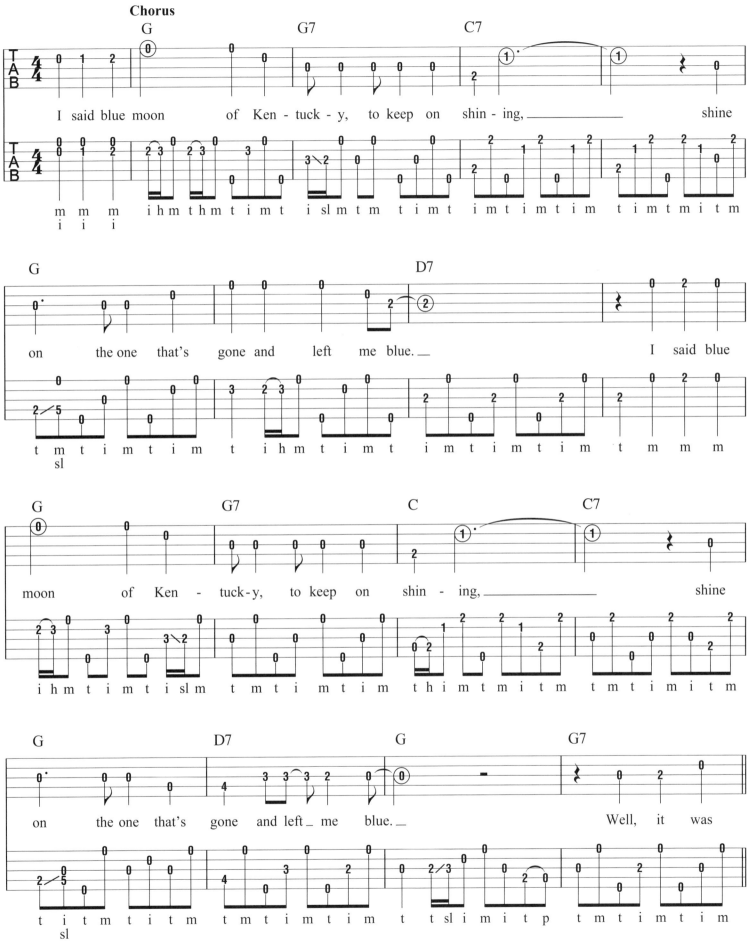

Bridge

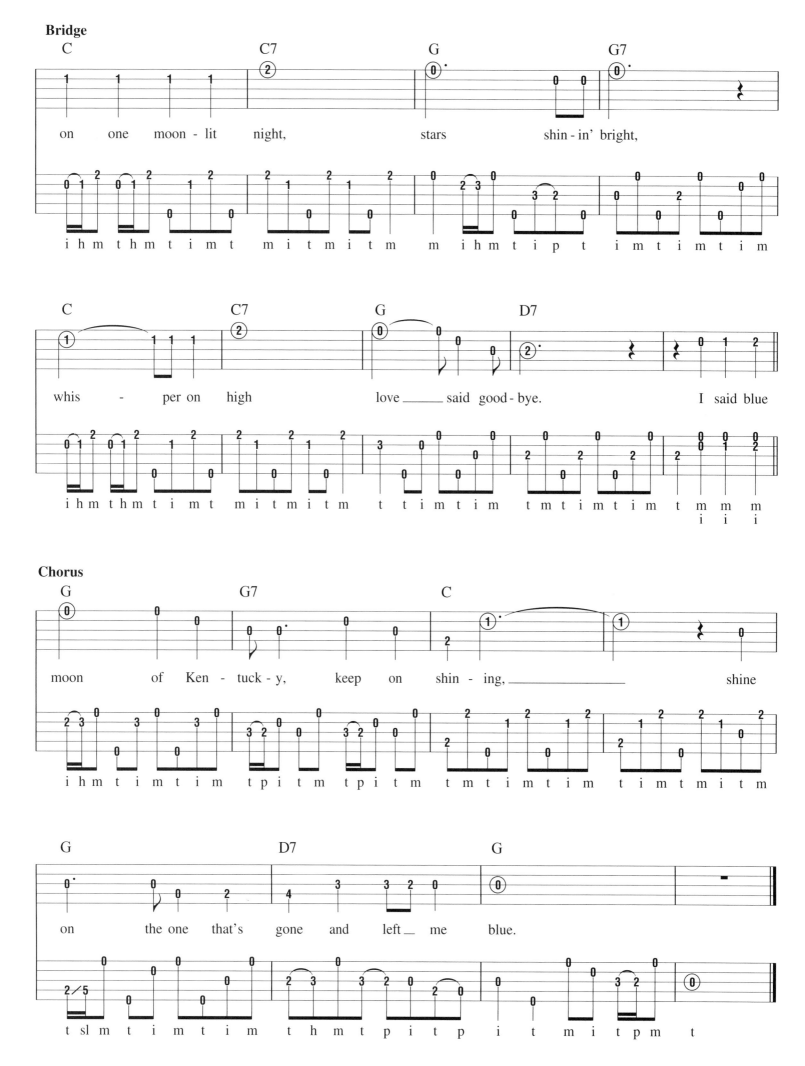

Chorus

SALTY DOG BLUES

Words and Music by Wiley A. Morris
and Zeke Morris

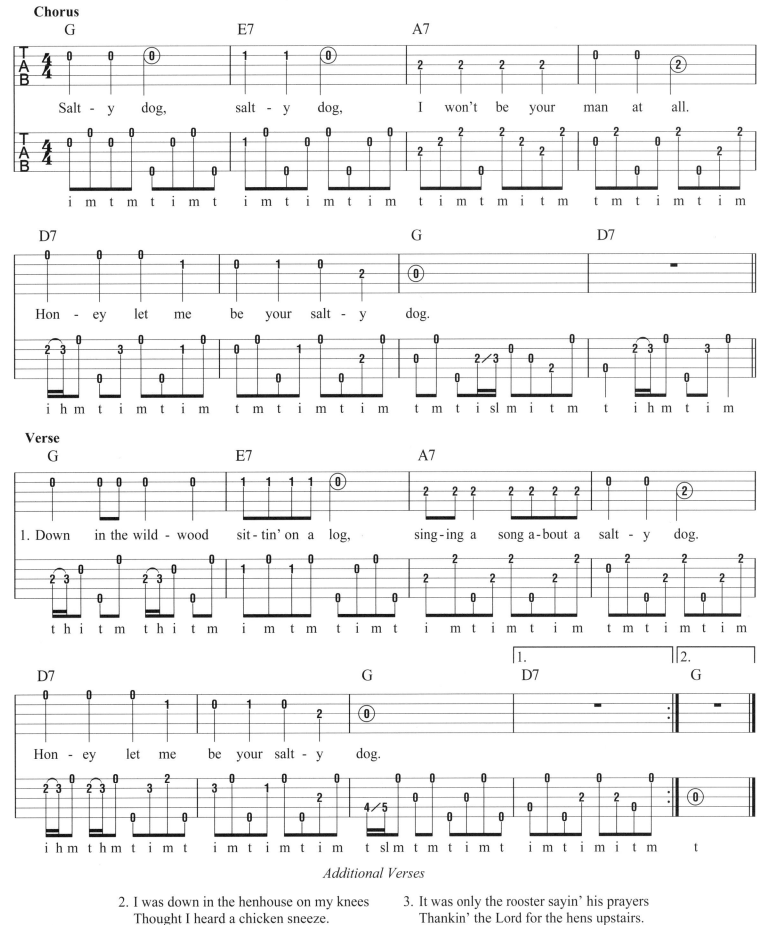

Additional Verses

2. I was down in the henhouse on my knees
   Thought I heard a chicken sneeze.
   Honey let me be your salty dog.

3. It was only the rooster sayin' his prayers
   Thankin' the Lord for the hens upstairs.
   Honey let me be your salty dog.

FOGGY MOUNTAIN BREAKDOWN

By Earl Scruggs

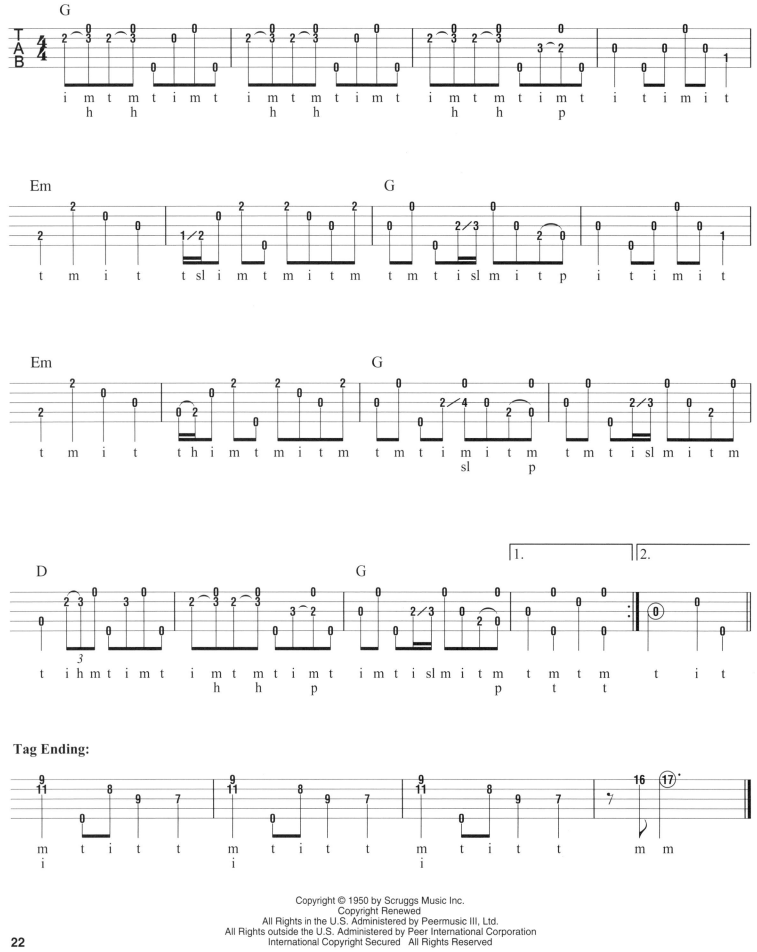

Tag Ending:

TEMPERENCE REEL

Traditional

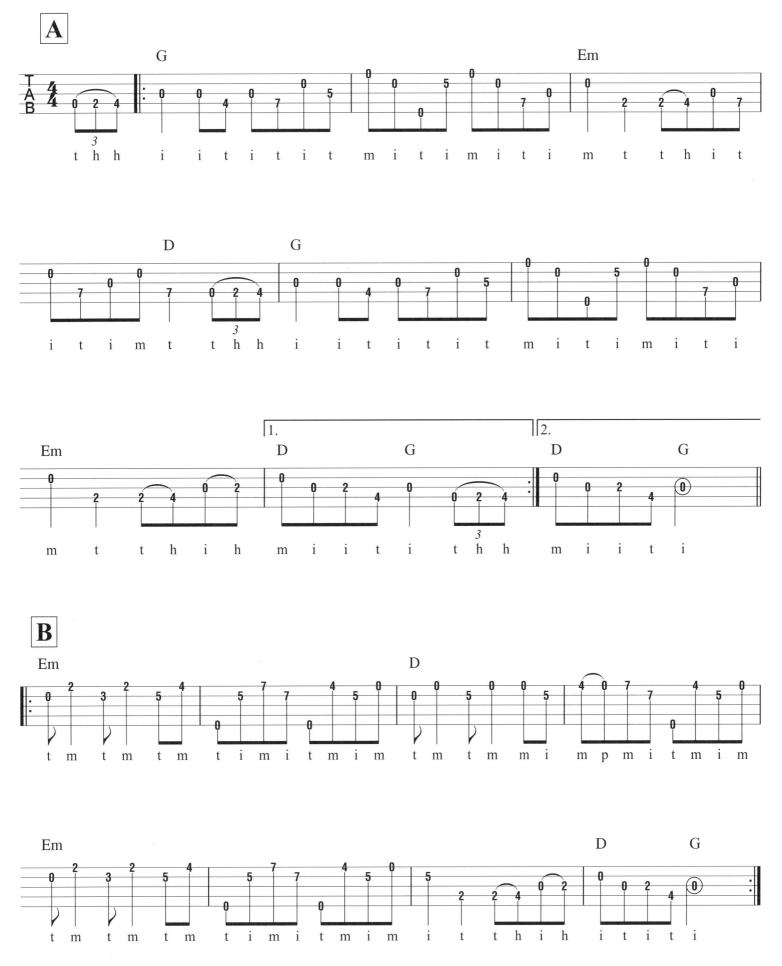

GREAT BANJO PUBLICATIONS

FROM HAL LEONARD CORPORATION

Hal Leonard Banjo Method – Second Edition

by Mac Robertson, Robbie Clement, Will Schmid
This innovative method teaches 5-string banjo bluegrass style using a carefully paced approach that keeps beginners playing great songs *while learning*. Book 1 covers easy chord strums, tablature, right-hand rolls, hammer-ons, slides and pull-offs, and more. Book 2 includes solos and licks, fiddle tunes, back-up, capo use, and more.
00699500 Book 1 (Book Only)... $7.99
00695101 Book 1 (Book/CD Pack) $16.99
00699502 Book 2 (Book Only $7.99

Banjo Chord Finder

This extensive reference guide covers over 2,800 banjo chords, including four of the most commonly used tunings. Thirty different chord qualities are covered for each key, and each chord quality is presented in two different voicings. Also includes a lesson on chord construction and a fingerboard chart of the banjo neck!

00695741 9 x 12... $6.99
00695742 6 x 9... $5.95

Banjo Scale Finder

by Chad Johnson
Learn to play scales on the banjo with this comprehensive yet easy-to-use book. It contains more than 1,300 scale diagrams for the most often-used scales and modes, including multiple patterns for each scale. Also includes a lesson on scale construction and a fingerboard chart of the banjo neck.

00695780 9 x 12... $6.95
00695783 6 x 9... $5.95

The Beatles for Banjo

18 of the Fab Four's finest for five string banjo! Includes: Across the Universe • Blackbird • A Hard Day's Night • Here Comes the Sun • Hey Jude • Let It Be • She Loves You • Strawberry Fields Forever • Ticket to Ride • Yesterday • and more.

00700813 ....$14.99

Christmas Favorites for Banjo

27 holiday classics arranged for banjo, including: Blue Christmas • Feliz Navidad • Frosty the Snow Man • Grandma's Killer Fruitcake • A Holly Jolly Christmas • I Saw Mommy Kissing Santa Claus • It's Beginning to Look like Christmas • Jingle-Bell Rock • Nuttin' for Christmas • Rudolph the Red-Nosed Reindeer • Silver Bells • and more.

00699109 .... $10.95

Fretboard Roadmaps

by Fred Sokolow
This handy book/CD pack will get you playing all over the banjo fretboard in any key! You'll learn to: increase your chord, scale and lick vocabulary • play chord-based licks, moveable major and blues scales, melodic scales and first-position major scales • and much more! The CD includes 51 demonstrations of the exercises.
00695358 Book/CD Pack $14.95

O Brother, Where Art Thou?

Banjo tab arrangements of 12 bluegrass/folk songs from this Grammy-winning album. Includes: The Big Rock Candy Mountain • Down to the River to Pray • I Am a Man of Constant Sorrow • I Am Weary (Let Me Rest) • I'll Fly Away • In the Jailhouse Now • Keep on the Sunny Side • You Are My Sunshine • and more, plus lyrics and a banjo notation legend.

00699528 Banjo Tablature.. $12.95

Earl Scruggs and the 5-String Banjo

Earl Scruggs' legendary method has helped thousands of banjo players get their start. It features everything you need to know to start playing, even how to build your own banjo! Topics covered include: Scruggs tuners • how to read music • chords • how to read tablature • anatomy of Scruggs-style picking • exercises in picking • 44 songs • biographical notes • and more! The CD features Earl Scruggs playing and explaining over 60 examples!
00695764 Book Only.. $19.95
00695765 Book/CD Pack $34.99

The Tony Trischka Collection

59 authentic transciptions by Tony Trischka, one of the world's best banjo pickers and instructors. Includes: Blown Down Wall • China Grove • Crossville Breakdown • Heartlands • Hill Country • Kentucky Bullfight • A Robot Plane Flies over Arkansas • and more. Features an introduction by Béla Fleck, plus Tony's comments on each song. Transcriptions are in tab only.

00699063 Banjo Tablature... $19.95

The Ultimate Banjo Songbook

A great collection of banjo classics: Alabama Jubilee • Bye Bye Love • Duelin' Banjos • The Entertainer • Foggy Mountain Breakdown • Great Balls of Fire • Lady of Spain • Orange Blossom Special • (Ghost) Riders in the Sky • Rocky Top • San Antonio Rose • Tennessee Waltz • UFO-TOFU • You Are My Sunshine • and more.

00699565 Book/2-CD Pack $24.95

FOR MORE INFORMATION, SEE YOUR LOCAL MUSIC DEALER, OR WRITE TO:

HAL•LEONARD® CORPORATION
7777 W. BLUEMOUND RD. P.O. BOX 13819 MILWAUKEE, WI 53213

Visit Hal Leonard online at **www.halleonard.com**

0514